everyday
happiness

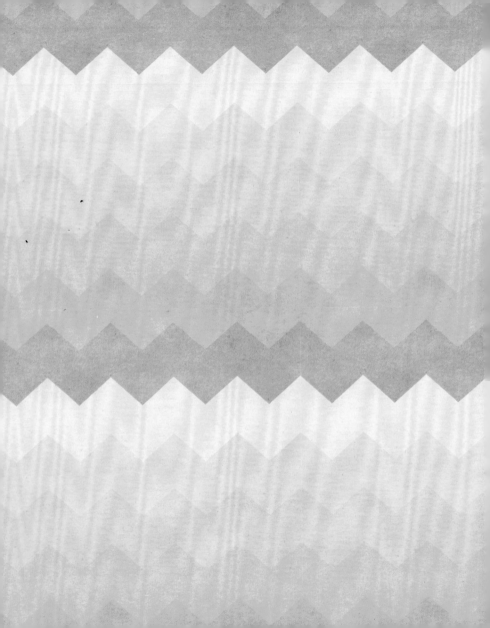

everyday happiness

365 WAYS TO A JOYFUL LIFE

Bounty
Books

An Hachette UK Company
www.hachette.co.uk

First published in 2016 by Bounty Books,
a division of Octopus Publishing Group Ltd
Carmelite House
50 Victoria Embankment
London, EC4Y 0DZ
www.octopusbooks.co.uk

ISBN: 978-0-75373-103-1

A CIP catalogue record for this book is available
from the British Library

Printed and bound in China

10 9 8 7 6 5 4 3 2

Design: Wide Open Studio
Publisher: Samantha Warrington
Design manager: Megan van Staden
Contributing editor: Emma Hill
Editor: Phoebe Morgan
Production controller: Caroline Alberti
Images: Shutterstock/Irtsya

INTRODUCTION

Happiness (noun):
1. The quality or state of being happy.
2. Good fortune; pleasure; contentment; joy.

Increasingly, scientists and philosophers are exploring what happiness is and how we can achieve it. If happiness were a formula, it would perhaps look something like this:

Gratitude + love + mindfulness
+ achievable goals = happiness

…with variations coloured by subjective opinion. One thing most happiness researchers do seem to agree on is that happiness is a choice; something that comes from within and that you can strive to achieve, regardless of your circumstances.

Everyday Happiness provides the perfect pick-me-up for days when you're in need of a positive boost.

Here you will find an eclectic mix of inspirational quotes; some are life affirming, others thought provoking or joyous, but all of them promote happiness.

Along with these daily inspirations are ideas and exercises to help you cultivate contentment.

Many of these tips involve taking just a few minutes out of your day, yet it's these small steps taken each day that will help set you on the path to happiness.

Use this book as your guide, inspiration and motivation to make this your happiest year yet.

MAKE A GRATITUDE JAR

Decorate an empty jar, to be filled throughout the year with notes about good things that happen. Don't let these good things pass by unnoticed, however small they may be.

"It's a helluva start, being able to recognise what makes you happy."

– LUCILLE BALL

"It isn't what you have, or
who you are, or where you are,
or what you are doing that
makes you happy or unhappy.
It is what you think about."

— DALE CARNEGIE

"We tend to forget that happiness doesn't come as a result of getting something we don't have, but rather of recognising and appreciating what we do have."

– FREDERICK KEONIG

EXERCISE

Exercise increases endorphins and other feel-good brain chemicals, so get moving today. Research suggests that the mood benefits of just 20 minutes of exercise can last for 12 hours. In fact exercise has such a profound effect on our happiness and wellbeing that it is an effective strategy for overcoming depression.

"Some cause happiness wherever they go; others whenever they go."

– OSCAR WILDE

"A man cannot
be comfortable
without his own
approval."

– MARK TWAIN

"Happiness is not something ready-made. It comes from your own actions."

– DALAI LAMA

REMEMBER, MONEY CAN'T BUY HAPPINESS

Research shows that once income climbs above the poverty level, more money brings very little extra happiness. Yet still so many of us strive to accumulate monetary wealth. This pursuit of 'stuff' will never bring enduring happiness.

"Very little is needed to make a happy life; it is all within yourself, in your way of thinking."

— MARCUS AURELIUS

"Twenty years from now you will be more disappointed by the things that you didn't do than by the ones you did do. So throw off the bowlines. Sail away from the safe harbour. Catch the trade winds in your sails. Explore. Dream. Discover."

– MARK TWAIN

"If you spend your whole life waiting for the storm, you'll never enjoy the sunshine."

– MORRIS WEST

"Most people are about as happy as they make up their minds to be."

– ABRAHAM LINCOLN

SLEEP MORE

We all know that sleep helps the body to repair itself, increases focus and concentration, but did you know it also plays an important role in happiness? Scientific studies have proven that sleep affects our sensitivity to negative emotions. So if you want to be more resilient, get an early night.

"To be kind to all, to like many and love a few, to be needed and wanted by those we love, is certainly the nearest we can come to happiness."

– MARY STUART

"Happiness consists of living each day as if it were the first day of your honeymoon and the last day of your vacation."

– LEO TOLSTOY

"I believe compassion to be one of the few things we can practice that will bring immediate and long-term happiness to our lives."

– DALAI LAMA

"Each morning when I open my eyes I say to myself: I, not events, have the power to make me happy or unhappy today. I can choose which it shall be. Yesterday is dead, tomorrow hasn't arrived yet. I have just one day, today, and I'm going to be happy in it."

– GROUCHO MARX

SPEND TIME WITH FAMILY

Top of the list of regrets expressed late in life is not spending enough time with family. Quality family time together is one major key to happiness.

"A table, a chair, a bowl of fruit and a violin; what else does a man need to be happy?"

– ALBERT EINSTEIN

"This planet has – or rather had – a problem, which was this: most of the people living on it were unhappy for pretty much all of the time. Many solutions were suggested for this problem, but most of these were largely concerned with the movement of small green pieces of paper, which was odd because on the whole it wasn't the small green pieces of paper that were unhappy."

– DOUGLAS ADAMS

GET OUTSIDE

Make the time to go outdoors today, even if just for 20 minutes in your lunch break. Studies show that fresh air boosts positivity and improves happiness levels.

"Life is really simple, but we insist on making it complicated."

– CONFUCIUS

GET IN TOUCH WITH AN OLD FRIEND

Why not contact an old friend who you haven't seen for a while? Don't let good friendships slip away just because life is busy. Make the effort to take ten minutes out of your day to write an email or a letter, or pick up the phone.

"If more of us valued food and cheer and song above hoarded gold, it would be a merrier world."

– J.R.R. TOLKIEN

"Thousands of candles can be lighted from a single candle, and the life of the candle will not be shortened. Happiness never decreases by being shared."

– BUDDHA

"A well-developed sense of humour is the pole that adds balance to your steps as you walk the tightrope of life."

– WILLIAM ARTHUR WARD

EXPRESS YOURSELF

Many of us suppress our feelings in order to keep the peace with others. This is so restrictive and can lead to a mediocre existence. Have the strength to express your feelings. Have the courage to live the life you want to.

"Learn to let go.
That is the key to
happiness."

– BUDDHA

"The grass is always greener where you water it."

– UNKNOWN

"The moments of happiness we enjoy take us by surprise. It is not that we seize them, but that they seize us."

– ASHLEY MONTAGU

HELP OTHERS

Hold open the door for someone, let a car out in traffic, deliver a homemade dinner to a friend, do some gardening for a neighbour in need, smile at a stranger... However small your gesture, it can make a huge difference to someone else's day, and the lovely side effect of this…you will feel happier!

"Don't cry
because it's over,
smile because it
happened."

– DR. SEUSS

"Count your age by friends, not years. Count your life by smiles, not tears."

– JOHN LENNON

"Happiness is not so much in
having as sharing. We make a living
by what we get, but we make a life
by what we give."

– NORMAN MACEWAN

"It is only possible to live happily ever after on a day to day basis."

— MARGARET BONANNO

SMILE

Several studies have shown that smiling may not just be an outward manifestation of a happy feeling. It may actually be able to cause a happy feeling.

"Sometimes your joy is the source of your smile, but sometimes your smile can be the source of your joy."

– THÍCH NHẤT HẠNH

Let yourself
be happy.

"All seasons are beautiful for the person who carries happiness within."

– HORACE FRIESS

HAPPINESS IS A CHOICE

The happiest people do not seek happiness in other people or possessions. They are not held hostage by circumstance. They understand that happiness comes from within and it is a choice. Today, whatever is going on in your life, choose happiness.

"The best way to cheer yourself is to try to cheer somebody else up."

– MARK TWAIN

"The foolish man seeks happiness in the distance, the wise grows it under his feet."

– JAMES OPPENHEIM

"The greatest part of our happiness depends on our dispositions, not our circumstances."

– MARTHA WASHINGTON

"The grand essentials of happiness are: something to do, something to love, and something to hope for."

- ALLAN K. CHALMERS

BE GRATEFUL

Let gratitude be your first thought in the morning and your last thought before you go to bed.

"For every minute
you are angry, you
lose sixty seconds
of happiness."

– RALPH WALDO EMERSON

"Be yourself;
everyone else is
already taken."

– OSCAR WILDE

SURROUND YOURSELF WITH HAPPY PEOPLE

Happiness is catching – being around contented people boosts your own mood. And by being happy yourself, you give something back to them. One big reciprocal circle of happy.

"You will never be happy if you
continue to search for what
happiness consists of.
You will never live if you are
looking for the meaning of life."

– ALBERT CAMUS

PLAN A TRIP

Even if you can't go on holiday for a while, plan ahead for a time when you can. It's often the anticipation of a positive event – not the event itself – that makes us happiest.

"Well," said Pooh, "What I like best," and then he had to stop and think. Because although eating honey was a very good thing to do, there was a moment just before you began to eat it which was better than when you were, but he didn't know what it was called."

– A.A. MILNE

"When one door of happiness closes, another opens; but often we look so long at the closed door that we do not see the one which has been opened for us."

– HELEN KELLER

"When all your desires are distilled;
You will cast just two votes:
To love more,
And be happy."

– RUMI

"The summit of happiness is reached when a person is ready to be what he is."

– DESIDERIUS ERASMUS

MEDITATE

Rewire your brain for happiness by meditating. Meditation clears the mind and calms you. It is often cited as the single most effective way to live a happier life.

"The pursuit of happiness is a most ridiculous phrase; if you pursue happiness you'll never find it."

– C. P. SNOW

"Those who bring sunshine into the lives of others, cannot keep it from themselves."

– JAMES M. BARRIE

TRY SOMETHING NEW

Challenge and novelty are key elements of happiness. Do something today that you've never done before.

"Your happiness
is a gift because it
literally brings out
the best in you."

– ROBERT HOLDEN

"Happiness depends upon ourselves."

– ARISTOTLE

"That is happiness;
to be dissolved
into something
completely great."

– WILLA CATHER

"We all live with the objective of being happy; our lives are all different and yet the same."

– ANNE FRANK

"Every morning, when we wake up, we have twenty-four brand new hours to live. What a precious gift! We have the capacity to live in a way that these twenty-four hours will bring peace, joy and happiness to ourselves and others."

– THÍCH NHẤT HẠNH

"Happiness is letting go of what you think your life is supposed to look like and celebrating it for everything that it is."

– MANDY HALE

"Happiness is like a butterfly; the more you chase it, the more it will elude you, but if you turn your attention to other things, it will come and sit softly on your shoulder…"

– HENRY DAVID THOREAU

LIVE IN THE MOMENT

Take 10 minutes out of your day for a mindfulness meditation. Being mindful means living in the moment, noticing what's going on both within our minds and in our immediate surroundings. It involves a gentle, non-judgemental acceptance of thoughts.

"Do not look back on happiness or dream of it in the future. You are only sure of today; do not let yourself be cheated out of it."

– HENRY WARD BEECHER

"The best day of your life is the one on which you decide your life is your own. No apologies or excuses. No one to lean on, rely on, or blame. The gift is yours – it is an amazing journey – and you alone are responsible for the quality of it. This is the day your life really begins."

– BOB MOAWAD

"One gets a
bad habit of being
unhappy."

– GEORGE ELIOT

HUG

Today give someone a genuine warm hug.
They'll hug you back and you'll both feel great!

HAVE A LAUGH

Laughter improves health, mood and social skills and is now even used as a therapy (laughter yoga was started in Mumbai by Dr Madan Katarina, who is now happily running over 5,000 clubs worldwide). So raise those endorphin levels and have a good chuckle.

"You cannot live your life to please others. The choice must be yours."

– LEWIS CARROLL

DANCE

Dance with carefree abandon.
Dance like nobody's watching.
Dance until you're sweating.
Dance until you can't wipe the smile off your face.

"There is no such thing as a
problem without a gift for you
in its hands. You seek problems
because you need their gifts."

– RICHARD BACH

"If you want to be happy,
set a goal that commands your
thoughts, liberates your energy,
and inspires your hopes."

– ANDREW CARNEGIE

LISTEN

Instead of waiting to jump in to a conversation, slow down and really listen to what somebody is telling you. You will feel a better connection to the person you are talking to if you understand their views. And a better connection equals increased levels of contentment within a relationship.

"The supreme happiness of life is the conviction that we are loved."

– VICTOR HUGO

"It is not easy to find happiness in ourselves, and it is not possible to find it elsewhere."

– AGNES REPPLIER

"We can travel a long way and do many things, but our deepest happiness is not born from accumulating new experiences. It is born from letting go of what is unnecessary, and knowing ourselves to be always at home."

– SHARON SALZBERG

SURROUND YOURSELF BY PEOPLE YOU LOVE

Our happiness levels increase when we are in the presence of people we love, so spend as much time as possible with the people you love. Simple!

"Try to make at least one person happy every day, and then in ten years you may have made three thousand, six hundred and fifty persons happy, or brightened a small town by your contribution to the fund of general enjoyment."

– SYDNEY SMITH

"The good life, as I conceive it, is a happy life. I do not mean that if you are good you will be happy; I mean that if you are happy you will be good."

– BERTRAND RUSSELL

"Most of us would be upset if we were accused of being 'silly.' But the word 'silly' comes from the old English word 'selig,' and its literal definition is 'to be blessed, happy, healthy and prosperous.'"

– ZIG ZIGLAR

MAKE A GRATITUDE LIST

Today, write down three good things that happened to you. It doesn't matter how small a thing it was. Anything that made you feel good at the time or that you're grateful for. This is a great way to ground yourself in what you love about your life. Grateful people are inevitably more fulfilled, contented and happy.

"Happiness, it seems to me, consists of two things: first, in being where you belong, and second – and best – in comfortably going through everyday life, that is, having had a good night's sleep and not being hurt by new shoes."

– THEODOR FONTANE

"Ever since happiness heard your name, it has been running through the streets trying to find you."

– HAFIZ OF PERSIA

"I had rather have a fool to make me merry than experience to make me sad."

– WILLIAM SHAKESPEARE

"I've learned that people will forget what you said, people will forget what you did, but people will never forget how you made them feel."

– MAYA ANGELOU

FAKE IT 'TIL YOU FEEL IT

Feelings follow actions. Today, if you're feeling low, act cheery. If you feel anger towards somebody, do something thoughtful for them and notice how this softens your anger.

"If you look to others for fulfilment, you will never be fulfilled. If your happiness depends on money, you will never be happy with yourself. Be content with what you have; rejoice in the way things are. When you realize there is nothing lacking, the world belongs to you."

– LAO TZU

"Happiness can be found even in the darkest of times, when one only remembers to turn on the light."

- J. K. ROWLING

"Tension is who you think you should be, relaxation is who you are."

- CHINESE PROVERB

"The art of living lies less in eliminating our troubles than growing with them."

– BERNARD M. BARUCH

"For me it is sufficient to have a corner by my hearth, a book, and a friend, and a nap undisturbed by creditors or grief."

– ANDRÉS FERNÁNDEZ DE ANDRADA

FORGIVE

According to a rapidly growing body of research, holding a grudge and nursing grievances can affect physical as well as mental health. So learn how to forgive. Try to let go of past hurts. Move on with compassion in your heart and your head held high.

"Happiness cannot be travelled to, owned, earned, worn or consumed. Happiness is the spiritual experience of living every minute with love, grace, and gratitude."

– DENIS WAITLEY

"Happiness is not a station you arrive at, but a manner of travelling."

— MARGARET LEE RUNBECK

"Focus on the journey, not the destination. Joy is found not in finishing an activity but in doing it."

– GREG ANDERSON

"You never regret being kind."

– NICOLE SHEPHERD

AN ACT OF RANDOM KINDNESS

Maybe buy a stranger their coffee, let someone jump the queue ahead of you, send anonymous flowers, buy someone a lottery ticket… then revel in the warm glow it brings you.

"Forgiveness does not change the past, but it does enlarge the future."

– PAUL BOESE

"In our lives, change is unavoidable, loss is unavoidable. In the adaptability and ease with which we experience change, lies our happiness and freedom."

– BUDDHA

"Reflect upon your present blessings, of which every man has many – not on your past misfortunes, of which all men have some."

– CHARLES DICKENS

"He who lives in harmony with himself lives in harmony with the universe."

– MARCUS AURELIUS

DECLUTTER

Start with one room or area in your house and focus on decluttering. Your mind will feel calmer and clearer for having done this.

"If you want others to be happy, practice compassion. If you want to be happy, practice compassion."

– DALAI LAMA

"Happiness is not having what you want. It is appreciating what you have."

– UNKNOWN

"We make a living by what we get, we make a life by what we give."

– WINSTON CHURCHILL

"Happiness is the experience of loving life. Being happy is being in love with that momentary experience. And love is looking at someone or even something and seeing the absolute best in him, her or it. Love is happiness with what you see. So love and happiness really are the same thing...just expressed differently."

– ROBERT MCPHILLIPS

EMBRACE
THE POSITIVE

Focus on embracing everything positive that happens to you today, however small that thing may be. For anything negative that happens, turn it into a positive. There's always a new way of looking at something, a way to put a positive spin on it.

"There is no stress in the world, only people thinking stressful thoughts and then acting on them."

– WAYNE DYER

"There is only one thing more painful than learning from experience and that is not learning from experience."

– ARCHIBALD MACLEISH

"Anything in life that we don't accept will simply make trouble for us until we make peace with it."

– SHAKTI GAWAIN

"Do what you have always done and you'll get what you have always got."

– SUE KNIGHT

SING

Put your favourite music on and sing.
Sing loud.
Sing with abandon.

"No one is in control of your happiness but you; therefore, you have the power to change anything about yourself or your life that you want to change."

– BARBARA DE ANGELIS

"The greatest happiness is to transform one's feelings into action."

– MADAME DE STAËL

PLAY

Perhaps with a pet or a child. Let yourself be child-like and
have fun. Did you know that children smile on average
400 times a day compared to just 20 times a day for adults?
Take a leaf out of their book today.

"We don't stop playing because we grow old; we grow old because we stop playing."

– GEORGE BERNARD SHAW

"The amount of happiness that you have depends on the amount of freedom you have in your heart."

– THÍCH NHẤT HẠNH

COMPLIMENT

Everywhere you go today, look for opportunities to pay
compliments to others. Be genuine and sincere.

"The happiness of life is made up of the little charities of a kiss or a smile, a kind look, a heartfelt compliment."

– SAMUEL TAYLOR COLERIDGE

"Think of what you have rather than of what you lack. Of the things you have, select the best and then reflect how eagerly you would have sought them if you did not have them."

– MARCUS AURELIUS

"To be content means that you realise you contain what you seek."

– ALAN COHEN

"Happiness is where we find it, but very rarely where we seek it."

– J. PETIT-SENN

"Happiness is
a by-product
of an effort to
make someone
else happy."

– GRETTA BROOKER PALMER

BUY YOURSELF FLOWERS

…and pick up a second bunch for someone else, too.

"'I shall take the heart,' returned the Tin Woodman, 'For brains do not make one happy, and happiness is the best thing in the world.'"

– L. FRANK BAUM

"Look at everything as though you were seeing it either for the first or last time. Then your time on earth will be filled with glory."

– BETTY SMITH

"Optimist:
a person who
travels on nothing
from nowhere to
happiness."

– MARK TWAIN

CULTIVATE
OPTIMISM

Regularly experiencing positive emotions results in an upward spiral. So find joy, gratitude, contentment and inspiration in as many places as you can today. Then more will follow.

"The mind is its own place, and in itself can make a heaven of hell, a hell of heaven."

– JOHN MILTON

"In our daily lives, we must see that it is not happiness that makes us grateful, but the gratefulness that makes us happy."

– ALBERT CLARKE

"Expecting life to treat you well
because you are a good person
is like expecting an angry bull
not to charge because you are
a vegetarian."

– SHARI R. BARR

"Boredom is the feeling that everything is a waste of time... serenity, that nothing is."

– THOMAS SZASZ

ACCEPT YOURSELF FOR WHO YOU ARE

If you can do this you will be so much happier. So today, make yourself a promise that you will not compare yourself to anyone else. You will not dwell on your flaws. Make a list of all the positive things about your personality to remind yourself that you are a good, kind human being. Being kinder to yourself will hugely increase your wellbeing.

"I celebrate myself,
and sing myself."

– WALT WHITMAN

"Happiness is
a perfume you
cannot pour on
others without
getting a few drops
on yourself."

– RALPH WALDO EMERSON

"But what is
happiness except
the simple harmony
between a man and
the life he leads?"

– ALBERT CAMUS

TAKE A PLANT
TO WORK

People who have plants in their workplaces are said to be happier than those who don't, so adorn your desk with vegetation for a shortcut to satisfaction.

"Just living is not enough… one must have sunshine, freedom, and a little flower."

– HANS CHRISTIAN ANDERSEN

"Nobody really cares if you're miserable, so you might as well be happy."

– CYNTHIA NELMS

"Those who can laugh without cause have either found the true meaning of happiness or have gone stark raving mad."

– NORM PAPERNICK

LEARN TO ENJOY THE SIMPLE THINGS IN LIFE

…like savouring a piece of chocolate,
a walk in the sunshine,
the smile of a loved one…

"The only way to do great work is to love what you do. If you haven't found it yet, keep looking. Don't settle."

– STEVE JOBS

"It is in our darkest moments that we must focus on the light."

– ARISTOTLE ONASSIS

"Challenges are what make life interesting and overcoming them is what makes life meaningful."

– JOSHUA J. MARINE

MAKE A GOAL

Feeling good about the future is one of the keys to happiness. We all need goals to motivate us, so set one today. It should be challenging enough to excite you, but also achievable. Choosing an ambitious but realistic goal will give your life direction and bring a sense of accomplishment and satisfaction when you achieve it.

"If you don't like something, change it. If you can't change it, change your attitude. Don't complain."

– MAYA ANGELOU

"Accept responsibility for your life. Know that it is you who will get you where you want to go, no one else."

– LES BROWN

"The key question to keep asking is: are you spending your time on the right things? Because time is all you have."

– RANDY PAUSCH

FIND A WAY TO BOUNCE BACK

Recent studies suggest that resilience is actually something that can be learned. We all have times of stress or trauma in our lives. We can't stop these bad things from happening, but we can change how we react to them. Make the choice to respond in a way that protects your wellbeing.

"In the depth of winter, I finally learned that within me there lay an invincible summer."

– ALBERT CAMUS

"Nobody can go back and start a new beginning, but anyone can start today and make a new ending."

– MARIA ROBINSON

"After a while, you learn to ignore the names people call you and just trust who you are."

– TAKEN FROM *SHREK*

"Pleasure is spread through the earth, In stray gifts to be claimed by whoever shall find."

– WILLIAM WORDSWORTH

WRITE A THANK YOU NOTE

Not for receiving a gift, but just because.
Maybe to a good friend thanking them for
being in your life, your child's teacher, or a
shop assistant who has been particularly helpful…
It should be handwritten and heartfelt.

"Happiness often sneaks in through a door you didn't know you left open."

- JOHN BARRYMORE

"Happiness quite unshared can scarcely be called happiness; it has no taste."

– CHARLOTTE BRONTË

"Little by little,
a little becomes
a lot."

– TANZANIAN PROVERB

LEARN SOMETHING NEW

Learning something new exposes us to different ideas and helps us to stay curious and engaged. It also gives us a sense of accomplishment and helps boost our self-esteem. So whether it's joining a Spanish club or learning how to crochet, sign up today.

"It is never too late to be what you might have been."

– GEORGE ELIOT

"Man is fond of counting his troubles, but he does not count his joys. If he counted them up as he ought to, he would see that every lot has enough happiness provided for it."

– FYODOR DOSTOEVSKY

"Tranquil pleasures last the longest; we are not fitted to bear the burden of great joys."

– CHRISTIAN NESTELL BOVEE

NOTICE THE WORLD AROUND YOU

So many people get stuck in the destructive cycle of thinking that there must be more to life than this. Well, there is, and it's right in front you. Today, open your eyes to what's around you. On your walk to work, the shops or wherever you're going, look at the trees around you, the clouds in the sky, a leaf on a bush, the sound of birdsong, children laughing…wherever you are, there will be something beautiful to tune into.

"A truly happy person is one who can enjoy the scenery while on a detour."

– UNKNOWN

"And in the end it's not the years in your life that count. It's the life in your years."

– ABRAHAM LINCOLN

"If you're going
through hell,
keep going."

– WINSTON CHURCHILL

"Happiness held
is the seed;
happiness shared
is the flower."

– UNKNOWN

FLOWERBOMB YOUR STREET

Scatter wildflower seeds on any spare patches
of soil and wait for your road to bloom.

"Don't be pushed by your problems. Be led by your dreams."

– RALPH WALDO EMERSON

"Just as a cautious businessman avoids investing all his capital in one concern, so wisdom would probably admonish us also not to anticipate all our happiness from one quarter alone."

– SIGMUND FREUD

"Nothing external
to you has any
power over you."

– RALPH WALDO EMERSON

"The love and attention you always thought you wanted from someone else, is the love and attention you first need to give to yourself."

– BRYANT MCGILL

MASSAGE

Indulge in a soothing massage. It will reduce stress levels, help you to sleep better and generally improve your sense of wellbeing.

"Nourishing yourself in a way that helps you blossom in the direction you want to go is attainable, and you are worth the effort."

– DEBORAH DAY

"To experience peace does not mean that your life is always blissful. It means that you are capable of tapping into a blissful state of mind amidst the normal chaos of a hectic life."

– JILL BOLTE TAYLOR

"If opportunity
doesn't knock,
build a door."

– MILTON BERLE

"Real elation is when you feel you could touch a star without standing on tiptoe."

– DOUG LARSON

A RANDOM NOTE

Write someone a lovely random note. Maybe hide one in your husband's coat pocket, in your child's lunchbox, or write it on a post-it to stick to a colleague's computer.

"I would always rather be happy than dignified."

– CHARLOTTE BRONTË

"Be who you are and say what you feel because those who mind don't matter, and those who matter don't mind."

– DR. SEUSS

FIND YOUR PURPOSE

Having a sense of purpose brings meaning to your life. Today, spend time thinking about what yours is. It may be a vocational job, being a parent, having a spiritual faith. We will all have a different answer, but each of them will involve being connected to something bigger than ourselves.

"You are beautiful. Know this.
Anyone who tells you otherwise is
simply lying. You are beautiful."

– STEVE MARABOLI

"The greatest weapon against stress is our ability to choose one thought over another."

– WILLIAM JAMES

"No one can make you feel inferior without your consent."

– ELEANOR ROOSEVELT

"Because one believes in oneself, one doesn't try to convince others. Because one is content with oneself, one doesn't need others' approval. Because one accepts oneself, the whole world accepts him or her."

– LAO TZU

BE MINDFUL

Instead of worrying about what has been and what is yet to come, ground yourself in the present moment and appreciate what is right here, right now. Take three deep breaths and realise that you are here, you are alive and all is well. Notice your thoughts, but don't judge them. Let them float away as for five minutes you focus on your breathing and just "being."

"Give your stress wings, and let it fly away."

– TERRI GUILLEMETS

"Love yourself first, and everything else falls in line. You really have to love yourself to get anything done in this world."

– LUCILLE BALL

"One joy scatters a hundred griefs."

– CHINESE PROVERB

EMBRACE YELLOW

According to studies, yellow is the happiest colour, so bring some yellow into your life today. Maybe wear a yellow scarf, buy some cheering daffodils or eat custard!

"We are each gifted in a unique and important way. It is our privilege and our adventure to discover our own special light."

– MARY DUNBAR

"Be happy.
It's one way of
being wise."

– COLETTE

"Precisely the least, the softest, lightest, a lizard's rustling, a breath, a flash, a moment – a little makes the way of the best happiness."

– FRIEDRICH NIETZSCHE

"No one has
ever become poor
by giving."

– ANNE FRANK

SEND A BOOK

Recommend a book you loved to someone
who you know will love it too. Even better,
send it to them anonymously.

"No one is useless in this world who lightens the burdens of another."

– CHARLES DICKENS

"The fact is always obvious much too late, but the most singular difference between happiness and joy is that happiness is a solid and joy a liquid."

– J.D. SALINGER

"People are like stained-glass windows. They sparkle and shine when the sun is out, but when the darkness sets in their true beauty is revealed only if there is light from within."

– ELISABETH KÜBLER-ROSS

"Eden is that old fashioned House
We dwell in every day
Without suspecting our abode
Until we drive away…"

– EMILY DICKINSON

A HAPPY PICTURE

Today, upload a happy picture and make it your screensaver, or print it out and put it somewhere you'll see throughout the day. If you're feeling down, just look at the picture and focus on the happy feelings it gives you.

"There is no exercise better for the heart than reaching down and lifting people up."

- JOHN HOLMES

"We only have
what we give."

- ISABEL ALLENDE

"People don't notice whether it's winter or summer when they're happy."

– ANTON CHEKHOV

"My advice to you is not to inquire why or whither, but just enjoy your ice cream while it's on your plate."

– THORNTON WILDER

HAKUNA MATATA

Learn to let go of your regrets, mistakes and worries.
You'll release yourself from the past that holds you back.
Look to the future with a happy mind-set.
Remember, happiness is a choice.

"Cheerfulness is what greases the axles of the world. Don't go through life creaking."

– H.W. BYLES

"The search for happiness is unlike any other search, for we search last in the likeliest places."

– ROBERT BRAULT

"Happiness is a by-product of an effort to make someone else happy."

– GRETTA BROOKER PALMER

VOLUNTEER

Help out in a charity shop, work in a soup kitchen, raise funds for a local cause…Find a way to make a difference. The welcome side effect of doing this means you will feel happier in yourself.

"Wherever you go,
no matter what the
weather, always
bring your own
sunshine."

– ANTHONY J. D'ANGELO

"You yourself, as much as anybody in the entire universe, deserve your love and affection."

– BUDDHA

PAMPER
YOURSELF

Book a spa day or simply take a long, relaxing bubble bath.
Look after yourself – you deserve it.

"Enjoy the little things, for one day you may look back and realise they were the big things."

– ROBERT BRAULT

LEARN TO DANCE

Or learn a new dance. When your brain and body are engaged,
learning something new, you'll feel great.

"It is a poor heart that never rejoices."

– CHARLES DICKENS

"True happiness is born of letting go of what is unnecessary."

– SHARON SALZBERG

"Most of the shadows of this life are caused by standing in one's own sunshine."

– RALPH WALDO EMERSON

"There is pleasure in the pathless woods, there is rapture in the lonely shore, there is society where none intrudes, by the deep sea, and music in its roar; I love not Man the less, but Nature more."

– LORD BYRON

GET BACK
TO NATURE

Take some time out and surround yourself with nature.
Take a walk in the country, spend some time gardening
or swim in a lake. Whatever you do, connecting yourself
with the wider natural world will be incredibly good for
your sense of wellbeing.

"For my part
I know nothing
with any certainty,
but the sight of
the stars makes
me dream."

– VINCENT VAN GOGH

"To be happy, we must not be too concerned with others."

– ALBERT CAMUS

"The best thing one can do when it's raining is to let it rain."

– HENRY WADSWORTH LONGFELLOW

"You only live once, but if you do it right, once is enough."

– MAE WEST

PRACTICE YOGA

Many people believe that the most mood-enhancing exercise is yoga. It also reduces anxiety, stress and improves your immune system, all of which will result in greater happiness.

"Once we are destined to live out our lives in the prison of our mind, our duty is to furnish it well."

– PETER USTINOV

"Don't ask yourself what the world needs, ask yourself what makes you come alive. And then go and do that. Because what the world needs is people who have come alive."

– HOWARD WASHINGTON THURMAN

WAKE UP YOUR WAY

Most of us have to set alarm clocks because we have responsibilities: a workplace or a school to get to, or a waking child. That's probably not going to change. But that doesn't mean we have to lose control over our mornings in the process. Set your alarm clock for just a little bit earlier so you can establish your own morning routine. This ritual can be something as small as letting yourself wake up slowly, reading a few pages of a book, focusing on a short breathing meditation or listening to a favourite piece of music on your headphones. Starting the day on your own terms will make a huge difference to your state of mind for the rest of the day.

"Success is getting what you want, happiness is wanting what you get."

– INGRID BERGMAN

"To love oneself is the beginning of a life-long romance."

— OSCAR WILDE

"Try to be a rainbow in someone's cloud."

– MAYA ANGELOU

EMBELLISH YOUR TO-DO LIST

Add something more meaningful than your usual daily tasks and chores to your to-do list today. It doesn't have to be anything monumental and time-consuming, but it should be important in the real sense of the word. Maybe it's to smile more, to make the time to do a jigsaw with your child, to hug a friend, to strike up a conversation with someone who looks lonely or sad…

"Who looks
outside, dreams;
who looks inside,
awakes."

– CARL GUSTAV JUNG

"You must do the things you think you cannot do."

– ELEANOR ROOSEVELT

COMPLAIN CONSTRUCTIVELY

Whining over every little thing is obviously going to be detrimental to our mental health. However, if you can voice your concerns in a constructive manner, you can come up with an action plan for each complaint, reach a solvable conclusion and thereby boost your mood and self-esteem.

"I believe in pink. I believe that laughing is the best calorie burner. I believe in kissing, kissing a lot. I believe in being strong when everything seems to be going wrong. I believe that happy girls are the prettiest girls. I believe that tomorrow is another day and I believe in miracles."

– AUDREY HEPBURN

"Keep your face always toward the sunshine – and shadows will fall behind you."

– WALT WHITMAN

"Clouds come floating into my life, no longer to carry rain or usher storm, but to add colour to my sunset sky."

– RABINDRANATH TAGORE

LEARN THE ART OF ACCEPTANCE

Never waste your time wondering about what might have been. Get busy thinking about what still might be, and trusting that however it plays out, it will leave you glad that what might have been, never came to be.

"There are two ways of spreading light: to be the candle or the mirror that reflects it."

– EDITH WHARTON

"There are always flowers for those who want to see them."

– HENRI MATISSE

ACCOMPLISH A TASK

Choose one important task that you can accomplish today, and do the same each and every day. The satisfaction of constant, daily achievement will lift your spirits.

"Nothing is impossible. The word itself says, 'I'm possible.'"

–AUDREY HEPBURN

"If you can't fly then run, if you can't run then walk, if you can't walk then crawl, but whatever you do, you have to keep moving forward."

– MARTIN LUTHER KING JR.

"Being deeply loved by someone gives you strength, while loving someone deeply gives you courage."

– LAO TZU

"Sing like no one is listening, love like you've never been hurt, dance like nobody is watching, and live like it's heaven on earth."

– MARK TWAIN

LOVE

Keep an open heart.
Love for the sake of love,
not to receive it in return.
To love is to live.

"A flower cannot blossom without sunshine, and man cannot live without love."

– MAX MULLER

"Happiness is when what you think, what you say, and what you do are in harmony."

– MAHATMA GANDHI

"Life is 10 percent what you make it, and 90 percent how you take it."

– IRVING BERLIN

"Do not go where the path may lead; go instead where there is no path and leave a trail."

– RALPH WALDO EMERSON

LOOK FOR THE MEANING IN YOUR PAIN

We all encounter pain at some point in our lives. Look upon either your current or past pains and seek the benefits that have or may arise from them. At the very least, perseverance is being built. And most likely, an ability to comfort others in their pain is also being developed.

"Life isn't about finding yourself. Life is about creating yourself."

– GEORGE BERNARD SHAW

"Don't judge each day by the harvest you reap, but by the seeds you plant."

– ROBERT LOUIS STEVENSON

"I have found that if you love life, life will love you back."

– ARTHUR RUBINSTEIN

"A journey of a thousand miles begins with a single step."

– LAO TZU

TREAT OTHERS HOW YOU WOULD LIKE TO BE TREATED

Be conscious of all of your actions.
Life is a circle and what goes around, comes around.

"The reason people find it so hard to be happy is that they always see the past better than it was, the present worse than it is, and the future less resolved than it will be."

– MARCEL PAGNOL

"When one door closes, another opens; but we often look so long and so regretfully upon the closed door that we do not see the one which has opened for us."

– ALEXANDER GRAHAM BELL

"Live as if you were
to die tomorrow.
Learn as if you were
to live forever."

– MAHATMA GANHDI

"Do or Do Not.
There is no Try."

– YODA

WRITE A NOT-TO-DO-LIST

Time to recognize your daily bad habits and then focus on not doing them. Simply writing them down can really help you to shift away from negative behaviour patters. So, what not to do today? Maybe your list will include losing patience with a certain colleague, raising your voice in arguments or at your children, reaching for an unhealthy snack…

"You've got
to do your
own growing,
no matter
how tall your
grandfather was."

– IRISH PROVERB

"I urge you to please notice when you are happy, and exclaim or murmur or think at some point, 'if this isn't nice, I don't know what is.'"

– KURT VONNEGUT

"Only love matters in the bits and pieces of a person's life."

— WILLIAM TREVOR

"If you are irritated by every rub, how will you be polished?"

– RUMI

SAY SORRY

You know who to.

"Uncertainty is the only certainty there is, and knowing how to live with insecurity is the only security."

– JOHN ALLEN PAULOS

"The harder you fall, the higher you bounce."

– UNKNOWN

"Be helpful. When you see a person without a smile, give them yours."

– ZIG ZIGLAR

TAKE CAKES OR FRUIT IN FOR YOUR COLLEAGUES

Engender a spirit of generosity and openness by taking in food to share with your colleagues. It is bound to bring cheer to the most lacklustre of workplaces.

"Among those whom I like or admire, I can find no common denominator, but among those whom I love, I can; all of them make me laugh."

– W. H. AUDEN

MAKE SOMEONE LAUGH

Is there a better sound in the world? Tell a joke, recount a funny story, tickle your child…whatever it takes to elicit a giggle from someone. You've brightened someone's day just for a moment, and in doing so have brightened your own.

"That it will never come again is what makes life so sweet."

– EMILY DICKINSON

"The things you think are the disasters in your life are not the disasters really. Almost anything can be turned around: out of every ditch, a path, if you can only see it."

– HILARY MANTEL

"Dwell on the beauty of life. Watch the stars, and see yourself running with them."

– MARCUS AURELIUS

"It is only with the heart that one can see rightly, everything essential is invisible to the eye."

– ANTOINE DE SAINT-EXUPÉRY

TELL SOMEONE YOU LOVE THEM

Don't assume they know this, so there is no need for it to be voiced. There is always a need to remind someone they are loved.

"Love is
the greatest
refreshment
in life."

– PABLO PICASSO

"How wonderful it is that nobody need wait a single moment before starting to improve the world."

– ANNE FRANK

"I learned that courage was not the absence of fear, but the triumph over it."

– NELSON MANDELA

BANISH NEGATIVE THOUGHTS

Try writing down your negative thoughts on a piece of paper, and then throwing the piece of paper away. Research suggests that physically discarding your worries can actually lessen their hold over you.

"You are never too old to set another goal or to dream a new dream."

– C. S. LEWIS

"Life is a mirror, if you frown at it, it frowns back; if you smile, it returns the greeting."

– WILLIAM MAKEPEACE THACKERAY

"At one with the One, it didn't mean a thing besides a glass of Guinness on a sunny day."

– GRAHAM GREENE

"If the world seems cold to you, kindle fires to warm it."

– LUCY LARCOM

PICK UP LITTER

Wherever you are walking today, pick up any litter. You will accomplish a sense of wellbeing by making the vicinity a more pleasant place for you and everyone else to be in.

"We can do no great things, only small things with great love."

– MOTHER TERESA

"In the hour of adversity, be not without hope; for crystal rain falls from black clouds."

– NIZAMI GANJAVI

"Those who wish
to sing, always
find a song."

– SWEDISH PROVERB

"One's life has value so long as one attributes value to the life of others, by means of love, friendship, and compassion."

– SIMONE DE BEAUVOIR

BE OPEN TO NEW FRIENDSHIPS

You may well find that you are friends with people who are very similar to you – of a similar age and from a comparable background, with hobbies and interests in line with your own. Be open to forming new relationships with neighbours, colleagues, friends of friends…no matter who they appear to be. Their differences will enrich your life.

...BUT NEVER FORGET YOUR OLD FRIENDS

They are your roots. They have seen you laugh uncontrollably, cry over a broken heart and plenty of other unmentionables. They know the essence of you. Enduring friendships are precious and to be treasured, and those based on support, honesty and love will certainly bring happiness.

"There are only two ways to live your life. One is as though nothing is a miracle. The other is as though everything is a miracle."

– ALBERT EINSTEIN

"Happiness is your nature. It is not wrong to desire it. What is wrong is seeking it outside when it is inside."

– RAMANA MAHARSHI

"The way I see it, if you want the rainbow, you gotta put up with the rain."

– DOLLY PARTON

"The most precious
things in life are free;
Love... smile... hug...
share... dream."

– CHARLOTTE HILL

EAT WELL

Indulge in mood-boosting nutrients to improve your mental state as well as your physical wellbeing. Studies have suggested that happiness and mental wellbeing are highest among people who eat plenty of fruit and vegetables every day.

"Above all, be
the heroine of
your own life, not
the victim."

– NORA EPHRON

"Even the darkest night will end and the sun will rise."

– VICTOR HUGO

"We are all in the gutter, but some of us are looking at the stars."

– OSCAR WILDE

TAKE A POWER SNOOZE

Napping has been shown to reduce cortisol levels, thereby reducing stress levels. Less stress equals more happiness.

"Never put a sock
in a toaster."

– EDDIE IZZARD

"The pessimist sees difficulty in every opportunity. The optimist sees opportunity in every difficulty."

– WINSTON CHURCHILL

GO EASY ON YOURSELF

Instead of dwelling on your failures, focus on your strengths and achievements and what you value about yourself. A shift away from self-criticism will boost your self-esteem and lead to increased levels of happiness.

"Did you ever see an unhappy horse? Did you ever see a bird that had the blues? One reason why birds and horses are not unhappy is because they are not trying to impress other birds and horses."

– DALE CARNEGIE

"The one thing we can never get enough of is love. And the one thing we can never give enough of is love."

– HENRY MILLER

MAKE A HAPPY BOX

Fill a box with some of your favourite things, to be opened on
bad days to calm, soothe and cheer you up. Maybe this could
contain your favourite book, sweets, a piece of artwork you love,
indulgent bath oil, a photograph that makes you smile…

"Never chase love, affection or attention. If it isn't given freely by another person, it isn't worth having."

– UNKNOWN

BE PROACTIVE IN YOUR RELATIONSHIPS

Particularly in regards to your partner. There is plenty of evidence to suggest that relationships, particularly marriages, decline over time. Don't switch to autopilot mode. Make an effort to engage. Today and every day.

"Good friends, good books, and a sleepy conscience: this is the ideal life."

– MARK TWAIN

"That man is richest whose pleasures are cheapest."

– HENRY DAVID THOREAU

"Your mission:
Be so busy loving
your life that you
have no time for
hate, regret or
fear."

– KAREN SALMANSOHN

"There are as many nights as days, and the one is just as long as the other in the year's course. Even a happy life cannot be without a measure of darkness, and the word 'happy' would lose its meaning if it were not balanced by sadness."

– CARL JUNG

MASTER A SKILL

This is all about engaging your strengths. Find something that you can excel in and do it as often as possible. Research has consistently suggested that using strengths contributes to greater wellbeing.

"Stop looking for happiness in the same place you lost it."

– UNKNOWN

"Today is one of your millions of moments of bliss."

– KIMBERLEY BLAINE

"If you want happiness for an hour
— take a nap.
If you want happiness for a day
— go fishing.
If you want happiness for a year
— inherit a fortune.
If you want happiness for a lifetime
— help someone else."

– CHINESE PROVERB

"I've always believed in savouring the moments. In the end, they are the only things we'll have."

– ANNA GODBERSEN

Eat chocolate.

"Anything is good if it's made of chocolate."

– JOE BRAND

"Pause and remember — every situation in life is temporary. So, when life is good, make sure you enjoy and receive it fully. And when life is not so good, remember that it will not last forever and better days are on the way."

– JENNI YOUNG

"Happiness is always a choice. You can't wait for circumstances to get better. You have to create your own good fortune. So look for ways to be happy every day."

– JOEL OSTEEN

"Always remember that your present situation is not your final destination. The best is yet to come."

– UNKNOWN

"If you get the inside right, the outside will fall into place."

– ECKHART TOLLE

HAVE MEANINGFUL CONVERSATIONS

Try and steer away from chat about the weather in favour of longer, more thoughtful conversations. Talking on a deeper level about more profound subjects and ideas can lead to stronger connections within your relationships.

"Too often we underestimate the power of a touch, a smile, a kind word, a listening ear, an honest compliment, or the smallest act of caring, all of which have the potential to turn a life around."

– LEO BUSCAGLIA

"You only have so much emotional energy each day. Don't spend it on things that don't matter or on people who don't value you or your time. Be discerning."

– DI RISEBOROUGH

"We must be our own before we can be another's."

– RALPH WALDO EMERSON

ALTER YOUR PERSPECTIVE

Put yourself in someone else's shoes. How would they view the situation? Altering your perspective can have a really big impact on your overall happiness.

"Today is a perfect day to just be happy."

– UNKNOWN

"As I say yes to life, life says yes to me!"

– LOUISE HAY

"Don't go around saying the world owes you a living. The world owes you nothing. It was here first."

– MARK TWAIN

DON'T BE A PERFECTIONIST

Perfectionism is an illusion and the pursuit of it can be very damaging. Use the 60% rule: if your relationship, career, friendship… is about 60% right, you're doing well.

"Joy is the simplest form of gratitude."

– KARL BARTH

"The most important decision you make is to be in a good mood."

– VOLTAIRE

"Never, ever underestimate the importance of having fun."

– RANDY PAUSCH

PLAN A STREET PARTY

Foster a sense of community spirit by planning a street party. This is a great way to get to know your neighbours better. And to have some fun, of course.

"I believe that if life gives you lemons, you should make lemonade… And try to find somebody whose life has given them vodka, and have a party."

– RON WHITE

"The whole world can love you,
but that love will not make you
happy. What will make you happy
is the love coming out of you."

– DON MIGUEL RUIZ

ASK FOR HELP

Don't be afraid to ask for help when you need it. Far from being a sign of weakness, the ability to request support shows a strength of character. So whether you need someone to fix your computer, or someone to give you a hug, just ask.

"If you want your life to be different you have to start reacting to life differently."

– BRYANT MCGILL

"If you have a family that loves you, a few good friends, food on your table and a roof over your head, you are richer than you think."

– UNKNOWN

SLOW DOWN

In our busy lives it's very easy to forget that we are human beings, not human doings. Many of us rarely allow ourselves to just 'be.' Schedule in some 'nothing' time today. You will feel re-energised, recharged and a sense of having regained some control over your frenetic life.

"In the end, it's not going to matter how many breaths you took, but how many moments took your breath away."

– SHING XIONG

"Age is something
that doesn't
matter, unless you
are a cheese."

– LUIS BUNUEL

AGE HAS NOTHING TO DO WITH IT

Stop thinking that you are too old to do something.
You're not.

"Keep smiling, and one day life will get tired of upsetting you."

– UNKNOWN

"Be careful what you water your dreams with. Water them with worry and fear and you will produce weeds that choke the life from your dream. Water them with optimism and solutions and you will cultivate success. Always be on the lookout for ways to turn a problem into an opportunity for success. Always be on the lookout for ways to nurture your dream."

– LAO TZU

"Know yourself. Be yourself. Love yourself. Seek goodness and be goodness. Seek beauty and be beauty. Seek love and be love."

– BRYANT MCGILL

"Real happiness doesn't come from getting everything you want. It comes from sharing what you have with the people who matter."

– UNKNOWN

TELL SOMEONE THEY MEAN A LOT TO YOU

Be open with your emotions.
This will lead to more meaningful
relationships and friendships.

"Good friends
are like stars.
You don't always
see them, but
you know they're
always there."

– UNKNOWN

"As human beings, we all want to be happy and free from misery. We have learned that the key to happiness is inner peace. The greatest obstacles to inner peace are disturbing emotions such as anger, attachment, fear and suspicion, while love and compassion and a sense of universal responsibility are the sources of peace and happiness."

– DALAI LAMA

OBSERVE HAPPINESS IN OTHERS

We all like to think that we are unique and will forge our own path through life. These things are both true, but what makes someone else happy may well make us happy, too. Learning about someone else's experience is a great way for us to internally evaluate if we will enjoy it as well. So look around at the happiest people you know. What do they enjoy doing? Use them as your inspiration.

"Some people make you laugh
a little louder, smile a little
brighter and live life a little better.
Try to be one of those people."

– UNKNOWN

"When you start recognising that you're having fun, life can be delightful."

– JANE BIRKIN

"For what it's worth: it's never too late to be whoever you want to be. I hope you live a life you're proud of, and if you find that you're not, I hope you have the strength to start over."

— F. SCOTT FITZGERALD

"Mistakes are the stepping stones to wisdom."

– LEON BROWN

"When a new day begins, dare to smile gratefully!"

— STEVE MARABOLI

"Do not take life
too seriously.
You will never get
out of it alive."

– ELBERT HUBBARD

THE TOP FIVE REGRETS OF THE DYING

As witnessed by palliative care nurse, Bronnie Ware.

1. I wish I'd had the courage to live a life true to myself, not the life others expected of me.

2. I wish I hadn't worked so hard.

3. I wish I'd had the courage to express my feelings.

4. I wish I had stayed in touch with my friends.

5. I wish that I had let myself be happier.

EMPTY YOUR GRATITUDE JAR

The jar you chose on 1st January should now be filled with notes about the good things that happened throughout your year. Read through all of these and let them bring you perspective, remind you of happy times and fill you with hope for the year ahead.